To MAUREEN WITH LOVE.

JENNY FOUND THIS BOOK WHICH IS
ALL ABOUT BOURNEMOUTH AND
MANY OF THE PICTURES ARE 1955,
THE YEAR OF THE "DEADLY EARRING"

PAGE 39 IS SPECIAL AS YOU CAN
SEE YOURSELF AND JENNY ON THE
NUMBER 29 RUSHING DOWN TO THE
SQUARE (THE IN PLACE TO MEET)

HAPPY BIRTHDAY FROM THE DUNK'S

SEPTEMBER 2004.

Francis Frith's
AROUND BOURNEMOUTH

PHOTOGRAPHIC MEMORIES

Francis Frith's
AROUND BOURNEMOUTH

◆

John Bainbridge

THE FRANCIS FRITH COLLECTION

FRITH BOOK Co

First published in the United Kingdom in 2000 by
Frith Book Company Ltd

Hardback Edition 2000
ISBN 1-85937-067-5

Paperback Edition 2002
ISBN 1-85937-545-6

British Library Cataloguing in Publication Data

Francis Frith's Around Bournemouth
John Bainbridge

Frith Book Company Ltd
Frith's Barn, Teffont,
Salisbury, Wiltshire SP3 5QP
Tel: +44 (0) 1722 716 376
Email: info@francisfrith.co.uk
www.francisfrith.co.uk

Printed and bound in Great Britain

AS WITH ANY HISTORICAL DATABASE THE FRITH ARCHIVE IS CONSTANTLY BEING CORRECTED AND IMPROVED
AND THE PUBLISHERS WOULD WELCOME INFORMATION ON OMISSIONS OR INACCURACIES

CONTENTS

FRANCIS FRITH: *Victorian Pioneer*

FRANCIS FRITH, Victorian founder of the world-famous photographic archive, was a complex and multitudinous man. A devout Quaker and a highly successful Victorian businessman, he was both philosophic by nature and pioneering in outlook.

By 1855 Francis Frith had already established a wholesale grocery business in Liverpool, and sold it for the astonishing sum of £200,000, which is the equivalent today of over £15,000,000. Now a multi-millionaire, he was able to indulge his passion for travel. As a child he had pored over travel books written by early explorers, and his fancy and imagination had been stirred by family holidays to the sublime mountain regions of Wales and Scotland. 'What a land of spirit-stirring and enriching scenes and places!' he had written. He was to return to these scenes of grandeur in later years to 'recapture the thousands of vivid and tender memories', but with a different purpose. Now in his thirties, and captivated by the new science of photography, Frith set out on a series of pioneering journeys to the Nile regions that occupied him from 1856 until 1860.

INTRIGUE AND ADVENTURE

He took with him on his travels a specially-designed wicker carriage that acted as both dark-room and sleeping chamber. These far-flung journeys were packed with intrigue and adventure. In his life story, written when he was sixty-three, Frith tells of being held captive by bandits, and of fighting 'an awful midnight battle to the very point of surrender with a deadly pack of hungry, wild dogs'. Sporting flowing Arab costume, Frith arrived at Akaba by camel seventy years before Lawrence, where he encountered 'desert princes and rival sheikhs, blazing with jewel-hilted swords'.

During these extraordinary adventures he was assiduously exploring the desert regions bordering the Nile and patiently recording the antiquities and peoples with his camera. He was the first photographer to venture beyond the sixth cataract. Africa was still the mysterious 'Dark Continent', and Stanley and Livingstone's historic meeting was a decade into the future. The conditions for picture taking confound belief. He laboured for hours in his wicker dark-room in the sweltering heat of the desert, while the volatile chemicals fizzed dangerously in their trays. Often he was forced to work in remote tombs and caves

where conditions were cooler. Back in London he exhibited his photographs and was 'rapturously cheered' by members of the Royal Society. His reputation as a photographer was made overnight. An eminent modern historian has likened their impact on the population of the time to that on our own generation of the first photographs taken on the surface of the moon.

VENTURE OF A LIFE-TIME

Characteristically, Frith quickly spotted the opportunity to create a new business as a specialist publisher of photographs. He lived in an era of immense and sometimes violent change. For the poor in the early part of Victoria's reign work was a drudge and the hours long, and people had precious little free time to enjoy themselves.

Most had no transport other than a cart or gig at their disposal, and had not travelled far beyond the boundaries of their own town or village. However, by the 1870s, the railways had threaded their way across the country, and Bank Holidays and half-day Saturdays had been made obligatory by Act of Parliament. All of a sudden the ordinary working man and his family were able to enjoy days out and see a little more of the world.

With characteristic business acumen, Francis Frith foresaw that these new tourists would enjoy having souvenirs to commemorate their days out. In 1860 he married Mary Ann Rosling and set out with the intention of photographing every city, town and village in Britain. For the next thirty years he travelled the country by train and by pony and trap, producing fine photographs of seaside resorts and beauty spots that were keenly bought by millions of Victorians. These prints were painstakingly pasted into family albums and pored over during the dark nights of winter, rekindling precious memories of summer excursions.

THE RISE OF FRITH & CO

Frith's studio was soon supplying retail shops all over the country. To meet the demand he gathered about him a small team of photographers, and published the work of independent artist-photographers of the calibre of Roger Fenton and Francis Bedford. In order to gain some understanding of the scale of Frith's business one only has to look at the catalogue issued by Frith & Co in 1886: it runs to some 670

pages, listing not only many thousands of views of the British Isles but also many photographs of most European countries, and China, Japan, the USA and Canada – note the sample page shown above from the hand written *Frith & Co* ledgers detailing pictures taken. By 1890 Frith had created the greatest specialist photographic publishing company in the world, with over 2,000 outlets – more than the combined number that Boots and WH Smith have today! The picture on the right shows the *Frith & Co* display board at Ingleton in the Yorkshire Dales. Beautifully constructed with mahogany frame and gilt inserts, it could display up to a dozen local scenes.

POSTCARD BONANZA

◆

The ever-popular holiday postcard we know today took many years to develop. In 1870 the Post Office issued the first plain cards, with a pre-printed stamp on one face. In 1894 they allowed other publishers' cards to be sent through the mail with an attached adhesive halfpenny stamp. Demand grew rapidly, and in 1895 a new size of postcard was permitted called the

court card, but there was little room for illustration. In 1899, a year after Frith's death, a new card measuring 5.5 x 3.5 inches became the standard format, but it was not until 1902 that the divided back came into being, with address and message on one face and a full-size illustration on the other. *Frith & Co* were in the vanguard of postcard development, and Frith's sons Eustace and Cyril continued their father's monumental task, expanding the number of views offered to the public and recording more and more places in Britain, as the coasts and countryside were opened up to mass travel.

Francis Frith died in 1898 at his villa in Cannes, his great project still growing. The archive he created continued in business for another seventy years. By 1970 it contained over a third of a million pictures of 7,000 cities, towns and villages. The massive photographic record Frith has left to us stands as a living monument to a special and very remarkable man.

Frith's Archive: *A Unique Legacy*

FRANCIS FRITH'S legacy to us today is of immense significance and value, for the magnificent archive of evocative photographs he created provides a unique record of change in 7,000 cities, towns and villages throughout Britain over a century and more. Frith and his fellow studio photographers revisited locations many times down the years to update their views, compiling for us an enthralling and colourful pageant of British life and character.

We tend to think of Frith's sepia views of Britain as nostalgic, for most of us use them to conjure up memories of places in our own lives with which we have family associations. It often makes us forget that to Francis Frith they were records of daily life as it was actually being lived in the cities, towns and villages of his day. The Victorian age was one of great and often bewildering change for ordinary people, and though the pictures evoke an impression of slower times, life was as busy and hectic as it is today.

We are fortunate that Frith was a photographer of the people, dedicated to recording the minutiae of everyday life. For it is this sheer wealth of visual data, the painstaking chronicle of changes in dress, transport, street layouts, buildings, housing, engineering and landscape that captivates us so much today. His remarkable images offer us a powerful link with the past and with the lives of our ancestors.

TODAY'S TECHNOLOGY

Computers have now made it possible for Frith's many thousands of images to be accessed almost instantly. In the Frith archive today, each photograph is carefully 'digitised' then stored on a CD Rom. Frith archivists can locate a single photograph amongst thousands within seconds. Views can be catalogued and sorted under a variety of categories of place and content to the immediate benefit of researchers. Inexpensive reference prints can be created for them at the touch of a mouse button, and a wide range of books and other printed materials assembled and published for a wider, more general readership - in the next twelve months over a hundred Frith local history titles will be published! The

See Frith at www.francisfrith.co.uk

day-to-day workings of the archive are very different from how they were in Francis Frith's time: imagine the herculean task of sorting through eleven tons of glass negatives as Frith had to do to locate a particular sequence of pictures! Yet the archive still prides itself on maintaining the same high standards of excellence laid down by Francis Frith, including the painstaking cataloguing and indexing of every view.

It is curious to reflect on how the internet now allows researchers in America and elsewhere greater instant access to the archive than Frith himself ever enjoyed. Many thousands of individual views can be called up on screen within seconds on one of the Frith internet sites, enabling people living continents away to revisit the streets of their ancestral home town, or view places in Britain where they have enjoyed holidays. Many overseas researchers welcome the chance to view special theme selections, such as transport, sports, costume and ancient monuments.

We are certain that Francis Frith would have heartily approved of these modern developments, for he himself was always working at the very limits of Victorian photographic technology.

THE VALUE OF THE ARCHIVE TODAY

Because of the benefits brought by the computer, Frith's images are increasingly studied by social historians, by researchers into genealogy and ancestory, by architects, town planners, and by teachers and schoolchildren involved in local history projects. In addition, the archive offers every one of us a unique opportunity to examine the places where we and our families have lived and worked down the years. Immensely successful in Frith's own era, the archive is now, a century and more on, entering a new phase of popularity.

THE PAST IN TUNE WITH THE FUTURE

Historians consider the Francis Frith Collection to be of prime national importance. It is the only archive of its kind remaining in private ownership and has been valued at a million pounds. However, this figure is now rapidly increasing as digital technology enables more and more people around the world to enjoy its benefits.

Francis Frith's archive is now housed in an historic timber barn in the beautiful village of Teffont in Wiltshire. Its founder would not recognize the archive office as it is today. In place of the many thousands of dusty boxes containing glass plate negatives and an all-pervading odour of photographic chemicals, there are now ranks of computer screens. He would be amazed to watch his images travelling round the world at unimaginable speeds through network and internet lines.

The archive's future is both bright and exciting. Francis Frith, with his unshakeable belief in making photographs available to the greatest number of people, would undoubtedly approve of what is being done today with his lifetime's work. His photographs, depicting our shared past, are now bringing pleasure and enlightenment to millions around the world a century and more after his death.

BOURNEMOUTH – *An Introduction*

STANDING ON BOURNEMOUTH sea front on a summer's day, when it is most alive with the sight and sound of thousands of tourists and humming with motor traffic, it is hard to grasp that less than two hundred years ago there was little to be seen in this spot except miles of wild heathland, and no sounds but the cry of the birds and the murmur of the sea.

For Bournemouth is a town of recent origin. Had Mr Lewis Tregonwell decided to build his holiday home elsewhere in 1810, there is a possibility that the Bournemouth we know today might never have existed. It was to take a further eighty years before this town even approached its heyday as a family seaside resort.

If anywhere should have become a resort it was neighbouring Mudeford, patronised as it was by regency notables such as Sir Walter Scott, Southey and Coleridge. But the flow of history, fortunately perhaps, passed Mudeford by; no doubt this was because of the iron-handed restrictions of the landowner of that time, Sir George Rose, who barely tolerated visitors unless they behaved with exceptional propriety.

No doubt seeking peace and quiet, other wealthy gentlemen followed Tregonwell's example; but even by 1841 there were still only some thirty houses scattered around the heathland. It was probably not until the arrival of the railway in 1870 that Bournemouth finally opened its doors to the mass invasion of tourists, many of whom subsequently took up residence. But that is not to say that a significant minority had not already discovered its considerable charms.

For many years the town catered for what the Victorians called 'the better class of visitor'; few others probably came, given the town's distance from the growing urban settlements. Local villagers and agricultural labourers would simply never have been able to afford the prices at the original hotels and boarding houses. Those who wandered into Bournemouth in pursuit of their trade must have been bewildered by the fineness and exclusivity of the strange new settlement.

Unlike resorts which had grown up around older industries such as fishing and merchant shipping, Bournemouth dedicated itself from the start as a venue for holiday pleasures, spurred on by the enterprising Sir George Gervis, a wealthy landowner who had arrived soon after Tregonwell. Under his guidance the first real hotels began to appear, a library and reading room were established, and the first villas - available for hire at four guineas a week - began to line the clifftops. An early travel writer approved: 'the magic hand of enterprise has converted the silent and unfrequented vale into the gay resort of fashion, and the favoured retreat of the invalid'.

But the whole project might still have foundered had it not been for the timely arrival of the famous Dr Granville, connoisseur of favoured watering places and eventual author of the standard Victorian guide to their health benefits, 'Spas of England and Principal Sea-Bathing Places'. Bournemouth's wily planners gave a dinner in the good doctor's honour, seeking his help in keeping the momentum going. Granville responded magnificently, announcing that the resort was superb for the treatment of consumption, but urging the gathered dignitaries not to allow the burgeoning new town to go downmarket.

On his advice the flowing waters of the Bourne Stream were captured and transformed into the tamer, decorative water feature we see today. The wilder parts of the vale were turned into gardens and walkways. Villas sprang up along the slopes of the hills and the clifftops, each one standing in its own health-giving grounds - just as the doctor ordered. Grateful valetudinarians, but only those who could afford to come, flooded into the area. The results were probably conducive to better health even if, as the consumptive Robert Louis Stevenson put it some years later, life there 'was as monotonous as a weevil's in a biscuit'.

As time went by and social attitudes changed, people arrived in Bournemouth for the sake of enjoyment alone. A wider choice of hotels and boarding houses became available. A pier was constructed, and a theatre and beach entertainments were provided. To cater for the huge increase in population and the massive influx of tourists, a huge variety of shops opened. Bournemouth's character evolved to something close to the one it has today.

This is not to say that it plunged rapidly downmarket. It continued to attract very well-heeled visitors: hotel advertisements of the 1890s boasted the patronage of the Prince of Wales (later Edward VII), the Empress of Austria, the King of the Belgians, Empress Eugenie - 'and all the leading Personages visiting Bournemouth'. A wider section of society enjoys Bournemouth today, for leaving aside its own delights and fascinating social history, it could have been tailor-made as a touring centre for Dorset and Hampshire. The new City of Bournemouth, together with Christchurch and Poole, makes up the largest urban mass on the Dorset coast.

Despite some modern buildings and the vast sprawl of its suburbs, this is still essentially a resort that Gervis and Granville would recognise - though the snobbish doctor would probably not approve of the influx of 'ordinary people' who come back year after year to enjoy the long miles of beaches or to linger in the flower-filled gardens.

Bournemouth is a part of the holiday memories of millions of Britons and travellers from further afield, a proud city and now a university town. These photographs, taken at important staging posts in its history, give us some idea of how the transformation from wild heathland to bustling resort came about.

FROM SOUTHBOURNE TERRACE c1870 5500

Bournemouth, once in Hampshire but now in Dorset, did not exist two hundred years ago. In 1810, Lewis Tregonwell built a holiday home on lonely heathland, close to the mouth of the tiny River Bourne. Other wealthy gentlemen followed his example, but it was to be the middle of that century before the town achieved popularity as a holiday resort.

SOUTHBOURNE TERRACE c1871 9664

Sir George Gervis, a rich landowner, added to Tregonwell's vision and founded Bournemouth as a fashionable resort. Advertisements of the day commented that 'enterprise has converted the silent and unfrequented vale into the gay resort of fashion, and the favoured retreat of the invalid'.

THE ARCADE c1871 5511

As with so many seaside resorts of the 19th century, Bournemouth attracted a wealthy and fashionable clientele. Shopkeepers were not long in seeing the business potential of catering for both residents and visitors. Shops and arcades were opened around the town, such as the impressive example of Victorian architecture seen above.

THE ARCADE c1955 B163153

The Arcade's interior was as lavish as the exterior. By the time this photograph was taken it had served the town well for around a century. The shopping arcade was very much a Victorian concept, enabling the shopper to browse without getting wet on rainy days.

THE PAVILION c1875 8089

The Victorians also developed the idea of building with glass to the furthest possible extent. The design of this glass pavilion owed a great deal to the influence of the Crystal Palace, built 25 years earlier to house the Great Exhibition.

SOUTHBOURNE TERRACE c1875 8082

SOUTHBOURNE TERRACE c1875
Not all invalid visitors were completely
captivated by the sprawling health resort.
Some were critical of the dryness of the
company. Robert Louis Stevenson
thought that life in Bournemouth was
'as monotonous as a weevil's in a
biscuit', and spent much of his time here
writing 'Kidnapped' and 'Dr Jekyll
and Mr Hyde'.

◆

ST PETER'S CHURCH 1887
The fine tower and spire of St Peter's
Church dominated much of central
Bournemouth, until unkind planners
allowed the construction of too many
large buildings nearby. This was the site
of the original parish church until it was
replaced in the 1840s. Mary Shelley, the
author of 'Frankenstein', is buried in the
churchyard with the heart of her
husband, Percy Bysshe Shelley.

ST PETER'S CHURCH 1887 19561

St Peter's Church c1955

This dramatic church was designed by the celebrated Victorian architect George Edmund Street, who also planned London's Law Courts. Buried within is the town's first vicar, Alexander Morden Bennett, who devoted much of his life to the promotion of Christianity in the resort.

◆

The Gardens 1890 25502

Bournemouth's Square stands at the very heart of the town, astride the Bourne Stream. Since its early days the resort has striven to be the 'Garden City by the Sea', and its lovely flower displays are a famous attraction for visitors.

St Peter's Church c1955 B163026

The Gardens 1890 25502

GENERAL VIEW 1904 52873
This fine skyline view of Edwardian Bournemouth,
with its wealth of splendid church buildings, is a
testimony to the endeavours of Bournemouth's first
vicar and his son Alexander Sykes Bennett, who
carried on his father's good works.

FROM THE SQUARE 1900 45214

A great effort was made to tame the wild landscape across which Bournemouth grew up. The Bourne Stream was rapidly transformed into an attractive water feature forming the centre point of the town. The Square was created on its banks.

THE SQUARE 1900 45215

A horse-drawn bus pauses in the Square around a century ago. Years ago it used to be said that if you lingered here long enough, everyone you knew would pass by sooner or later.

THE SQUARE 1904 52875
Bournemouth had the first electric trams in England, though it eventually gave them up in favour of electric
trolley-buses. The old tramlines were eventually torn up and used to reinforce the concrete of the sea wall.

THE SQUARE 1900 45218
Like so many seaside resorts of the period,
Bournemouth attracted a wealthy clientele who built
numerous villas for permanent and semi-permanent
occupation. Here we see the carriages of the well-to-do
assembled in the Square in 1900.

THE SQUARE 1923 74782
By the 1920s Bournemouth had become a major south coast resort, rivalling Brighton and Torquay. The traffic in the Square increased accordingly, with private motor cars competing with the charabanc for parking spaces. The latter would take trippers to the many beautiful localities nearby, such as Purbeck and the New Forest.

THE SQUARE AND THE GARDENS 1925 78777

In 1925 the Square was beginning to show the degree of traffic problems that were to blight the town in future years. As well as being a holiday resort, Bournemouth was gaining a reputation as a smart shopping town, and by this time department stores were lining the main streets. The gardens around the Square provided a pleasant refuge from the hurly-burly of 20th-century life - they still do, in this new century.

THE SQUARE c1955 B163031

By the 1950s motor traffic was beginning to dominate the centre of Bournemouth, though it was still possible for drivers to easily pull in at the side of the road. The family holiday enjoyed something of a revival in the fifties as rationing and austerity came to an end.

THE SQUARE C1955 B163027

Chain and department stores arrived early in Bournemouth, though a large number of family owned shops survived until the end of the 20th century. Many shoppers came to the town every week from distant places to do their weekly shopping.

THE SQUARE C1955 B163030

By the time this photograph was taken, Bournemouth was at the height of its popularity as this view of the town centre shows. In high summer it became difficult to find an available bed in the resort's many hotels and guest houses.

THE TOWN CENTRE c1955 B163110
As the 20th century progressed, Bournemouth abandoned any pretence of being a health resort, embracing the idea of being a holiday resort par excellence. Virtually every shop, hotel and visitor facility was designed or adapted to achieve that end.

THE CENTRE C1955 B163148

THE CENTRE c1955

Today the great conurbation that is Bournemouth has absorbed older settlements nearby and has linked up with the ancient towns of Christchurch and Poole. About a third of Dorset's population now lives within the area, and Bournemouth has achieved city status.

TOWN CENTRE c1960

One reason for Bournemouth's success as a holiday resort has been that the shops are available if the weather is too wet and windy for the beach. Public transport came early to Bournemouth, making the town a superb central location for visitors wishing to explore the locality.

TOWN CENTRE c1960 B163084

THE PLEASURE GROUNDS 1900 45220
Few resorts have as many green spaces as Bournemouth; these are the remnants of the original great chine and wild heathland around which the town was built. Most of these are now formal gardens, where it is possible to stroll, watch the entertainments or just sit and relax.

INVALID'S WALK 1900 45225
Bournemouth and the neighbouring towns became a sanctuary for the rich and famous, including writers such as Mary Shelley and Robert Louis Stevenson. Royal visitors included the Empress Eugenie, the King of the Belgians and Edward VII - who discreetly entertained his mistresses Lilly Langtry and Mrs Keppel at a hotel on the East Cliff.

THE GARDENS 1904 52877
It is hard to imagine the wild and deserted heathland of a century earlier when you look at this crowded and formal scene, with properly laid-out gardens, high buildings and a tamed stream.

THE BANDSTAND 1933 85609
Visitors and residents alike gather around the bandstand to hear one of the many bands - military or civilian - which play on summer afternoons. Bournemouth has long been associated with music. Its famous Symphony Orchestra often gives concerts at the nearby Winter Gardens.

PAVILION GARDENS c1955 B163154

Many of the trees in the various pleasure gardens were planted in Victorian times to 'improve the air quality' on the advice of the influential Dr Granville. He gave the town's planners many similar ideas on how Bournemouth's potential as a health resort could be best realised.

THE METROPOLE HOTEL 1900 45227

Luxury hotels were built to cater for the better-heeled visitor to Bournemouth, which prospered well into the 20th century. Some early tourists would hire villas and bring their entire family and retinue of servants with them.

THE GRAND HOTEL 1895 35085
Even in a class-ridden Victorian society, Bournemouth entertained anyone who could afford to stay in the town. The variety of accommodation ranged from hotels such as the Metropole and Grand down to family boarding houses, commercial lodgings and public houses.

PARKSTONE, SANDECOTES 1900 46098
The suburbs of Bournemouth, which have now sprawled out into the neighbouring countryside, began with the early construction of villa residences, each with its own garden - as suggested by Dr Granville - along the back of the clifftops and on the slopes above the Bourne Stream.

WESTOVER ROAD C1955

Westover Road, with its clear-cut and dramatic lines, runs from the direction of the sea to the square; it is still an important shopping street. The trolley-bus cables, seen top left, have long gone.

RICHMOND HILL C1955

The Bournemouth Echo is the town's evening newspaper, founded in 1900. Its striking building is seen here in the centre of the picture. Unlike many similar local newspapers, it has survived to the present day at its Richmond Hill offices.

WESTOVER ROAD C1955 B163020

RICHMOND HILL C1955 B163025

Along The Seashore

IT IS DIFFICULT to calculate just when humanity's love affair with the seaside began. Prehistoric man may have journeyed to the seashore in search of salt and shellfish, but his journey was probably strictly utilitarian. Generations of Britons -island dwellers all - certainly lived with the surrounding waters, exploiting them for fishing and often as a perilous transport route. But how many experienced the desire to linger there is unclear.

Holidays and rest cures probably began with the major expansion of the spa towns from the 17th century onwards. A hundred years later physicians suggested that salt water might be as beneficial to health as the mineral waters of the exclusive spa resorts. The British began to dip their toes in the sea, so to speak. King George III did much to popularise the activity at Weymouth: he dived into the water whilst a discreetly hidden band played 'God Save the King'. The seaside resort had come of age.

As we have seen, Bournemouth was a late starter in this scheme of things. Mr Lewis Tregonwell built his house there in 1810, probably more because his wife liked the ambience of the area than for its sea bathing qualities, though the several miles of adjacent beaches must have been a great temptation.

Bournemouth's first bathers were a mixture of the prudish and the daring. One early visitor reported that shy paddlers '...bob about from dell to dell as if they thought that every bush concealed a serpent or a tempting apple'. Braver souls plunged into the briny with nothing on at all, for nude bathing was commonplace until late into the 19th century. One tourist, William Miller, was outraged not by the nude bathing but by the behaviour of bystanders, and commented that 'the forwardness of the women makes it unpleasant for the bathers. For not content with gazing down from the cliffs above, they are often passing by or near the bathers. I think the visitors to Bournemouth are more shameless than at any other place'. So much for Victorian prudery!

Whether or not the consumptives, who had come to Bournemouth on the advice of Dr Granville and his ilk, took to the sea as part of their cure is hard to say. It is more likely that they enjoyed bracing walks along the beach and Undercliff, or sat admiring the flowers in the pleasure gardens instead.

It took the arrival of popular tourism before all those miles of golden beaches were exploited to their full potential. It was pressure from a wider class of holidaymaker that led to the use of the pier as a recreational resource, rather than just an anchorage for shipping, and to the construction of promenades, swimming baths and theatres. Through most of the 20th century, traditional seaside holidays shaped Bournemouth; millions of Britons must have spent at least one holiday here at some point in their lives.

Competition from foreign holidays dented the profits of the town for some years, though there seems to have been a renaissance in family holidays recently. Bournemouth's potential as a touring centre and a location for short breaks is now being properly realised, and the city's future as a place to visit looks assured. On good summer days, the beaches of Bournemouth seem as crowded as at any time in the resort's short but exciting history.

SANDBANKS, THE HOTEL 1900 46102
Sandbanks is the long spit of land dividing Poole Harbour from the sea at the southwestern end of Bournemouth. This once lonely stretch of coast has been developed somewhat since this photograph was taken; it marks the beginning of Bournemouth's long stretch of coastline.

SANDBANKS 1904 52797
Sandbanks gives an impression of how wild and lonely the nearby site of Bournemouth must have been before Lewis Tregonwell built his house there in 1810. With Poole Harbour beyond, and Brownsea Island in view, this long peninsula is an excellent place to watch wildfowl.

ALUM CHINE 1925 78781
Alum Chine, with its spectacular coastal scenery, became a popular walk down to the seashore for visitors staying in the family hotels of Westbourne. This photograph shows very clearly the reluctance to build too near the edge of these unstable cliffs.

DURLEY CHINE 1925 78782

The natural scenery of the Bournemouth coastline dictated the way the new town developed. Many of the chines, the wild ravines which split the cliff line, were quickly adapted as pleasure grounds and scenic walks down to the beach.

EAST CLIFF STEPS 1908 61185

Apart from the areas around the mouth of the Bourne Stream, much of Bournemouth was built to the rear of the long line of cliffs, necessitating many stairways down to the beach for energetic visitors. The cliff lift - signposted from here - was available for the lazier tourist.

WEST CLIFF LIFT 1908

Cliff lifts became a popular solution to the problems of beach access in the later years of the Victorian period, and were used at a number of seaside resorts. The West Cliff Lift may not have had to cope with the long gradient of some others, but was a masterpiece of mechanical design nevertheless.

THE CLUB HOUSE c1871

The Victorian Club House was built to make some gesture to the needs of tourists, though not all 19th-century visitors were impressed. The Victorian guide book writer J Burney Yeo complained that the new town had 'no esplanade or promenade' and found the burgeoning resort very dull in comparison with others.

WEST CLIFF LIFT 1908 61184

THE CLUB HOUSE c1871 5660

THE BEACH 1904 52880
But despite Mr Yeo's discouraging comments,
Bournemouth flourished; by Edwardian times it was
one of England's leading resorts, with visitors
cramming the long miles of beaches. Despite the
resort's early reputation for nude bathing, all of the
tourists seen here seem overdressed - even by the
standards of 1904!

FROM THE PIER c1871 5661
Bournemouth's Pier stands above the original mouth of the Bourne Stream. Its construction marked the town's commitment to its role as a resort. The mildness of the climate first attracted visitors to the town, and it rapidly acquired a reputation as a place beneficial to consumptives. Note the boy sweeping the sand away.

FROM THE PIER 1897 40559
Nearly a century after its foundation, the town was already dominating the skyline, and its beaches were among the most crowded on the south coast. Thomas Hardy had described the town as 'Sandbourne' in his novel 'The Hand of Ethelberta' and immortalised it in 'Tess of the D'Urbervilles' as 'the city of detached mansions'.

THE SWANAGE BOAT 1908 61183
Since this part of the coast had few harbours, most
of the coastal pleasure boats moored alongside
Bournemouth's piers. Here we see the Swanage
paddle steamer about to set off. Paddle steamers still
occasionally visit the resort.

51

THE PIER 1918 68064
This view shows a busy Bournemouth Pier attracting
strollers and sightseers. There are few men in this
picture taken in the last summer of the Great War -
though Bournemouth was a popular retreat for
soldiers on leave from the trenches.

THE PIER 1918 68065

Most seaside piers started out as purely functional structures, a way to allow boats and ships to moor off towns without a harbour. Victorian entrepreneurs soon became aware that people liked to walk out along them, and began to provide attractions and charge admittance.

THE PIER ENTRANCE 1918 68066

It is just after midday on a summer's day in 1918. War-weary visitors try to banish the horrors of the First World War for a few hours. A careful examination of the crowds shows a sprinkling of uniforms, though many of the men in the scene seem to have cast off their uniforms for 'mufti'.

THE PIER ENTRANCE 1925 70750

A busier view of Bournemouth's pier attracting the crowds. The pier has undergone several transformations since it was first built, but retains its popularity. By the twenties motor cars had almost completely replaced earlier horse drawn transport, and charabanc tours had become a popular feature of a seaside holiday.

THE PIER APPROACH c1955 B163012

Piers may have become more elaborate as the 20th century wore on, but the fundamental joy of walking above the waves never failed to appeal to human nature. On a clear day much of the wide sweep of the Hampshire coastline could be seen.

EAST CLIFF 1897 40562

This view of East Cliff, with well-clad visitors strolling along the beach, and sailing boats drawn up on the shore, shows a south coast beach before development and formalisation changed its character. Even so, as long ago as this the trappings of a modern seaside resort were starting to appear.

UNDERCLIFF DRIVE 1913 66117

Undercliff Drive runs the long distance eastwards from Bournemouth's Pier to the pier at Boscombe. Familiar to generations of holidaymakers, its wide pavement serves as one of the resort's most popular promenade walks.

UNDERCLIFF DRIVE 1922 72692
By the 1920s, promenaders along Undercliff Drive had to cope with a modest increase in motor traffic, though the majority of visitors preferred to walk or cycle. Chalets and beach huts were crammed into every available space at this time to fulfil the demand for them. Some were privately owned, and others rented out to holidaymakers.

East Cliff 1918 68069
Because of the unstable nature of the cliffs, many of
Bournemouth's buildings were built at a distance from
the cliff edge. Here we are looking across at East Cliff
from the rising gradient of West Cliff. The headlands
of Boscombe and Southbourne are in the background.

EAST CLIFF FROM THE WEST 1897 40556
High above the East Cliff promenade are the turrets
and flags of The Royal Bath Hotel, one of the town's
leading resorts at this time. Its advertisement boasted
patronage by '...the Prince of Wales, King of the
Belgians, the Empress Eugenie...and all the most
distinguished personages visiting Bournemouth'.

FROM WEST CLIFF 1922   72685
Looking back the other way we see West Cliff. Early visitors preferred to stay in the hotels and villas of this area, within easy walking distance of the sea. The parasols, shown in the photograph, were used to provide shade from the bright sun.

THE BATHS FROM BATH ROAD c1955
By the 20th century holiday resorts were catering for visitors during bad weather as well as good, hence the imposing public baths. It is worth comparing this photograph with earlier ones of the same site to see the dramatic changes.

◆

THE PAVILION AND THE BATHS c1955
By the 1950s the first high rise hotels had appeared; also, Bournemouth's old trams had given way to trolley-buses, hence the overhead lines. The public swimming baths, the Pavilion Theatre and an indoor bowling green showed the town's commitment to being an all-the-year-round resort.

THE BATHS FROM BATH ROAD c1955 B163015

THE PAVILION AND THE BATHS c1955 B163145

THE PAVILION c1955 B163146

The Pavilion Theatre and Ballroom was established in 1928, and has remained popular with visitors ever since. There are now several other venues for live entertainment in the town, including the Winter Gardens, home of the world-famous Bournemouth Symphony Orchestra. The newer Bournemouth International Centre, with its 3500 capacity auditorium, has now joined the Pier Theatre and the Wessex and Tregonwell Halls to make the city the entertainment capital of the south coast.

THE PAVILION c1955 B163143

As we look at this busy Bournemouth scene from the 1950s, it is hard to imagine that all this was a wild and barren heathland, deserted except for fishermen and smugglers, only 150 years before.

THE BEACH AND PIERS c1960 B163071

By the 1960s English resorts were having to compete with the lure of foreign holidays. Bournemouth fell back on the appeal of the traditional family holiday and short break seaside visits. It is interesting to see that paddle steamers, so familiar to the Victorians, were still plying their trade along this coast - and still do sometimes.

The Bordering Settlements

THERE CAN HARDLY be a greater contrast in both history and architecture than that between Christchurch and Bournemouth. The first is as ancient as the latter is modern. Christchurch Twyneham, to give this 'settlement between the two rivers' its full name, is a wonderful place which has managed to avoid being overwhelmed by its larger neighbour, retaining its important historic identity. The two rivers are the Stour and the Avon, which flow a considerable distance across the West Country before reaching the sea nearby. The added delights of river scenery and the old-fashioned estuary at Mudeford complement this old priory town.

Christchurch itself, which imposed its name on the older Saxon town round about, was once part of a greater historic priory which held much power and influence, owning a great many wealthy manors throughout Southern England. It is arguably the finest medieval church in a county of grand churches.

The Normans built the nearby castle to stamp their domineering authority on what had been an important Saxon burgh. But the fine church has survived where the castle has fallen, and the latter's ruins dominate the town much less than the ecclesiastical buildings, which in the end came to have more power over the local community. The town itself boasts a wonderful array of architecture, mostly Georgian and Victorian, and has happily been spared the worst excesses of 20th century intrusion. Christchurch is a lovely town to explore and to seek out its history and archaeology, legend and architecture.

Poole, too, has an ancient history, for it is situated on one of the few large natural harbours along this coast. It adopted resort status almost as an afterthought; it was already secure in its past as a mercantile centre. For centuries it was the largest town in the area, until Bournemouth's suburbs swept out to embrace its own.

The settlements of Boscombe and Southbourne give a first impression of having been totally absorbed by Bournemouth, rather in the way a cuckoo throws out the original inhabitants of the nest, but this is deceptive. Close investigation shows that each has preserved its unique identity.

Boscombe developed alongside Bournemouth, and achieved a certain popularity with the literary and artistic community in Victorian times. The discovery of a mineral spring in 1868 gave the fledgling community high hopes of becoming a spa town, but it never really took off; it devoted its communal energies instead to becoming a resort - complete with constructed sea front and pier. Its flower-filled gardens are one of the delights of the area in spring and summer. Southbourne, tucked away between sea and river, retains an air of quiet respectability even today. Its streets and buildings are a delight to the student of Victorian architecture, and there are peaceful walks by sea and inland water.

The bordering communities are more than just a happy complement to the great resort nearby. They are fascinating places to explore in their own right. The Frith photographers have revealed just a few of their many delightful scenes.

CHRISTCHURCH, THE PRIORY CHURCH 1890 25203

Legend relates that the original site for the priory church was on the nearby St Catherine's Hill, a splendid viewpoint overlooking the town. But each day work previously completed was undone and moved to the present site. A mysterious carpenter was observed miraculously raising the rafters with divine perfection, and the building was named Christ Church in his honour.

CHRISTCHURCH, THE CASTLE 1900 45050

Christchurch Castle, of which only the ruins remain, was probably built by Richard de Redvers, a cousin of Henry I, who was given the royal manor as a reward for aiding Henry in his fight for the crown following the death of William Rufus. In the Civil War the castle was captured in 1645 by Colonel Goring, who rendered the building indefensible.

CHRISTCHURCH, HIGH STREET 1900 45043
At the time of the Domesday Book there were already 21 houses in Christchurch, and 24 canons attached to the priory church. In medieval times the town prospered; the settlement was well-established at a time when the site of Bournemouth was still a wild heath. The High Street shows some splendid examples of Georgian and Victorian architecture; with the castle and priory, it would have been the focus of the ancient town for a thousand years.

CHRISTCHURCH, BLACKWATER FERRY 1900 45048

CHRISTCHURCH
Blackwater Ferry 1900

Christchurch stands on two rivers, the Stour and the Avon, and gets its original name Twyneham, or Tweoxneham, from the Anglo-Saxon meaning 'the town between the two rivers'. Here we see the ferryman at Blackwater pulling the ferry across the water by the very ancient method of using a rope as a means of propulsion.

POOLE
The Town Cellars 1887

Clustered alongside the harbour, the older part of Poole is well worth exploring. In the 19th century, the town had many independent breweries. The picture shows a horse-drawn brewer's dray outside the town cellars. The huge warehouse on the right gives clear evidence of the importance of Poole's mercantile past.

POOLE, THE TOWN CELLARS 1887 19511

POOLE, HIGH STREET 1900 40080

Poole developed alongside the finest natural harbour in England. It still maintains strong links with the sea, having become a mecca for yachtsmen. Here are some splendid examples of Victorian shop fronts. W J Bacon's general store has awnings and a covered walkway to protect customers from both sun and shower. Notice the coat of arms above the corner of the street.

POOLE, HARBOUR OFFICES 1904 52815

Near the quays is the 18th-century harbour office, once the Old Town House, a club for the sailing ships which docked nearby. On the front of the building is an ancient sundial, and on the right hand side a carving of Benjamin Skutt, Mayor of Poole in 1727.

POOLE, HIGH STREET 1908 61164
A busy midday street scene in Edwardian Poole, with horse-drawn carriages, cyclists and pedestrians still dominating the town. It is interesting that it was still possible for people to hold a conversation standing in the road, as the trio on the right seems able to do with little danger. Fashion and respectability demanded that everyone from the smallest child to the eldest shopper wore a hat.

POOLE, BARGES AT THE QUAY 1908 61171
Less than a century ago, sailing ships still dominate the quays at Poole. Ships' chandlers and coal merchants line the waterside, and a coal cart stands idle at the side of the road. The building on the middle left is the Customs House, whose officials would have worked around the clock checking vessels arriving from foreign ports for contraband and diseased passengers or crew.

CORFE MULLEN, THE OLD MILL TEA ROOMS c1955 C596005

Corfe Mullen is one of the largest parishes in Dorset, but until the middle of the 20th century it was a modest village. Now the suburbs of Poole have crept nearer, and the old village has become a small dormitory town. Corfe Mullen's mill received a mention in the Domesday Book. Here we see a very 1950s scene - the tea rooms combined with a petrol station catering for the revolution in popular motoring.

CORFE MULLEN, THE CHURCH c1955 C596018

Corfe Mullen stands on the alluvial flood plain of the River Stour, surrounded originally by the wild heathlands of south-east Dorset. Until well into the 20th century the nearby river would overflow the fields to the north of the village in a flood up to a mile wide. The parish church often stood just a road's width from the limit of the rising waters.

BOSCOMBE, THE ARCADE 1892 31380
Bournemouth rapidly absorbed the older settlements nearby, including Boscombe. But Boscombe's shops and arcades soon attracted visitors from its larger neighbour. The gothic architecture seen here remained an enthusiasm for builders and architects throughout much of the Victorian period.

BOSCOMBE, CHRISTCHURCH ROAD 1892 31381
Christchurch Road, seen here as it enters Boscombe,
must be one of the longest streets in England, as it runs
the full distance from Bournemouth to Christchurch.
This view gives some excellent examples of Victorian
shop signs; Endle's chemist shop has a gaslit illuminated
sign over the doorway, while the nearby cycle shop
boasts a penny-farthing to advertise its wares.

BOSCOMBE, FROM THE PIER 1906 55907
Boscombe developed to the east of Bournemouth in
mid-Victorian times, attracting the fashionable and
wealthy. Mineral springs added to Boscombe's
attractions for those seeking an improvement to
health, though it never became the spa
it aspired to be.

BOSCOMBE, THE PIER 1903 49156

BOSCOMBE
The Pier 1903

Paddle steamers arrive and depart from Boscombe's pier during its Edwardian heyday. The construction of a pier marked the town's determination to make its mark as a holiday resort, and not to be overshadowed by its larger neighbour. This structure, as with the pier at Bournemouth, was severely damaged during the Second World War, but both have been sympathetically restored. A third pier at Southbourne did not survive.

◆

SOUTHBOURNE
Fisherman's Walk 1922

Southbourne maintains its air of tranquillity even today, compared to the bustle of Bournemouth. It is bordered by the sea on one side and a meandering river on the other. The Fisherman's Walk, at Stourcliff, has been a popular access route to the coast and seashore for generations.

SOUTHBOURNE, FISHERMAN'S WALK 1922 72714

SOUTHBOURNE, STREET SCENE C1955 S153101

Until the area became too built-up, Southbourne was used by pioneer aviators as a landing ground for their flying machines. Mr Rolls, of Rolls Royce fame, has the unfortunate distinction of being the first pilot to die in a British air accident, when his fragile aeroplane crashed nearby.

WESTBOURNE, THE BEACH 1918 68071

Despite modern development, Westbourne, to the west of Bournemouth, retains its village atmosphere. Spacious houses and hotels are situated around a dramatic woodland chine leading down to the sea. Westbourne has some of the best clifftop views in the area, overlooking the broad waters of Poole Bay.

Index

Frith Book Co Titles

www.francisfrith.co.uk

The Frith Book Company publishes over 100 new titles each year. A selection of those currently available are listed below. For latest catalogue please contact Frith Book Co.

Town Books 96 pages, approx 100 photos. County and Themed Books 128 pages, approx 150 photos (unless specified). All titles hardback laminated case and jacket except those indicated pb (paperback)

Title	ISBN	Price	Title	ISBN	Price
Amersham, Chesham & Rickmansworth (pb)	1-85937-340-2	£9.99	Derby (pb)	1-85937-367-4	£9.99
Ancient Monuments & Stone Circles	1-85937-143-4	£17.99	Derbyshire (pb)	1-85937-196-5	£9.99
Aylesbury (pb)	1-85937-227-9	£9.99	Devon (pb)	1-85937-297-x	£9.99
Bakewell	1-85937-113-2	£12.99	Dorset (pb)	1-85937-269-4	£9.99
Barnstaple (pb)	1-85937-300-3	£9.99	Dorset Churches	1-85937-172-8	£17.99
Bath (pb)	1-85937-419-0	£9.99	Dorset Coast (pb)	1-85937-299-6	£9.99
Bedford (pb)	1-85937-205-8	£9.99	Dorset Living Memories	1-85937-210-4	£14.99
Berkshire (pb)	1-85937-191-4	£9.99	Down the Severn	1-85937-118-3	£14.99
Berkshire Churches	1-85937-170-1	£17.99	Down the Thames (pb)	1-85937-278-3	£9.99
Blackpool (pb)	1-85937-382-8	£9.99	Down the Trent	1-85937-311-9	£14.99
Bognor Regis (pb)	1-85937-431-x	£9.99	Dublin (pb)	1-85937-231-7	£9.99
Bournemouth	1-85937-067-5	£12.99	East Anglia (pb)	1-85937-265-1	£9.99
Bradford (pb)	1-85937-204-x	£9.99	East London	1-85937-080-2	£14.99
Brighton & Hove(pb)	1-85937-192-2	£8.99	East Sussex	1-85937-130-2	£14.99
Bristol (pb)	1-85937-264-3	£9.99	Eastbourne	1-85937-061-6	£12.99
British Life A Century Ago (pb)	1-85937-213-9	£9.99	Edinburgh (pb)	1-85937-193-0	£8.99
Buckinghamshire (pb)	1-85937-200-7	£9.99	England in the 1880s	1-85937-331-3	£17.99
Camberley (pb)	1-85937-222-8	£9.99	English Castles (pb)	1-85937-434-4	£9.99
Cambridge (pb)	1-85937-422-0	£9.99	English Country Houses	1-85937-161-2	£17.99
Cambridgeshire (pb)	1-85937-420-4	£9.99	Essex (pb)	1-85937-270-8	£9.99
Canals & Waterways (pb)	1-85937-291-0	£9.99	Exeter	1-85937-126-4	£12.99
Canterbury Cathedral (pb)	1-85937-179-5	£9.99	Exmoor	1-85937-132-9	£14.99
Cardiff (pb)	1-85937-093-4	£9.99	Falmouth	1-85937-066-7	£12.99
Carmarthenshire	1-85937-216-3	£14.99	Folkestone (pb)	1-85937-124-8	£9.99
Chelmsford (pb)	1-85937-310-0	£9.99	Glasgow (pb)	1-85937-190-6	£9.99
Cheltenham (pb)	1-85937-095-0	£9.99	Gloucestershire	1-85937-102-7	£14.99
Cheshire (pb)	1-85937-271-6	£9.99	Great Yarmouth (pb)	1-85937-426-3	£9.99
Chester	1-85937-090-x	£12.99	Greater Manchester (pb)	1-85937-266-x	£9.99
Chesterfield	1-85937-378-x	£9.99	Guildford (pb)	1-85937-410-7	£9.99
Chichester (pb)	1-85937-228-7	£9.99	Hampshire (pb)	1-85937-279-1	£9.99
Colchester (pb)	1-85937-188-4	£8.99	Hampshire Churches (pb)	1-85937-207-4	£9.99
Cornish Coast	1-85937-163-9	£14.99	Harrogate	1-85937-423-9	£9.99
Cornwall (pb)	1-85937-229-5	£9.99	Hastings & Bexhill (pb)	1-85937-131-0	£9.99
Cornwall Living Memories	1-85937-248-1	£14.99	Heart of Lancashire (pb)	1-85937-197-3	£9.99
Cotswolds (pb)	1-85937-230-9	£9.99	Helston (pb)	1-85937-214-7	£9.99
Cotswolds Living Memories	1-85937-255-4	£14.99	Hereford (pb)	1-85937-175-2	£9.99
County Durham	1-85937-123-x	£14.99	Herefordshire	1-85937-174-4	£14.99
Croydon Living Memories	1-85937-162-0	£9.99	Hertfordshire (pb)	1-85937-247-3	£9.99
Cumbria	1-85937-101-9	£14.99	Horsham (pb)	1-85937-432-8	£9.99
Dartmoor	1-85937-145-0	£14.99	Humberside	1-85937-215-5	£14.99
			Hythe, Romney Marsh & Ashford	1-85937-256-2	£9.99

Available from your local bookshop or from the publisher

Frith Book Co Titles (continued)

Title	ISBN	Price	Title	ISBN	Price
Ipswich (pb)	1-85937-424-7	£9.99	St Ives (pb)	1-85937415-8	£9.99
Ireland (pb)	1-85937-181-7	£9.99	Scotland (pb)	1-85937-182-5	£9.99
Isle of Man (pb)	1-85937-268-6	£9.99	Scottish Castles (pb)	1-85937-323-2	£9.99
Isles of Scilly	1-85937-136-1	£14.99	Sevenoaks & Tunbridge	1-85937-057-8	£12.99
Isle of Wight (pb)	1-85937-429-8	£9.99	Sheffield, South Yorks (pb)	1-85937-267-8	£9.99
Isle of Wight Living Memories	1-85937-304-6	£14.99	Shrewsbury (pb)	1-85937-325-9	£9.99
Kent (pb)	1-85937-189-2	£9.99	Shropshire (pb)	1-85937-326-7	£9.99
Kent Living Memories	1-85937-125-6	£14.99	Somerset	1-85937-153-1	£14.99
Lake District (pb)	1-85937-275-9	£9.99	South Devon Coast	1-85937-107-8	£14.99
Lancaster, Morecambe & Heysham (pb)	1-85937-233-3	£9.99	South Devon Living Memories	1-85937-168-x	£14.99
Leeds (pb)	1-85937-202-3	£9.99	South Hams	1-85937-220-1	£14.99
Leicester	1-85937-073-x	£12.99	Southampton (pb)	1-85937-427-1	£9.99
Leicestershire (pb)	1-85937-185-x	£9.99	Southport (pb)	1-85937-425-5	£9.99
Lincolnshire (pb)	1-85937-433-6	£9.99	Staffordshire	1-85937-047-0	£12.99
Liverpool & Merseyside (pb)	1-85937-234-1	£9.99	Stratford upon Avon	1-85937-098-5	£12.99
London (pb)	1-85937-183-3	£9.99	Suffolk (pb)	1-85937-221-x	£9.99
Ludlow (pb)	1-85937-176-0	£9.99	Suffolk Coast	1-85937-259-7	£14.99
Luton (pb)	1-85937-235-x	£9.99	Surrey (pb)	1-85937-240-6	£9.99
Maidstone	1-85937-056-x	£14.99	Sussex (pb)	1-85937-184-1	£9.99
Manchester (pb)	1-85937-198-1	£9.99	Swansea (pb)	1-85937-167-1	£9.99
Middlesex	1-85937-158-2	£14.99	Tees Valley & Cleveland	1-85937-211-2	£14.99
New Forest	1-85937-128-0	£14.99	Thanet (pb)	1-85937-116-7	£9.99
Newark (pb)	1-85937-366-6	£9.99	Tiverton (pb)	1-85937-178-7	£9.99
Newport, Wales (pb)	1-85937-258-9	£9.99	Torbay	1-85937-063-2	£12.99
Newquay (pb)	1-85937-421-2	£9.99	Truro	1-85937-147-7	£12.99
Norfolk (pb)	1-85937-195-7	£9.99	Victorian and Edwardian Cornwall	1-85937-252-x	£14.99
Norfolk Living Memories	1-85937-217-1	£14.99	Victorian & Edwardian Devon	1-85937-253-8	£14.99
Northamptonshire	1-85937-150-7	£14.99	Victorian & Edwardian Kent	1-85937-149-3	£14.99
Northumberland Tyne & Wear (pb)	1-85937-281-3	£9.99	Vic & Ed Maritime Album	1-85937-144-2	£17.99
North Devon Coast	1-85937-146-9	£14.99	Victorian and Edwardian Sussex	1-85937-157-4	£14.99
North Devon Living Memories	1-85937-261-9	£14.99	Victorian & Edwardian Yorkshire	1-85937-154-x	£14.99
North London	1-85937-206-6	£14.99	Victorian Seaside	1-85937-159-0	£17.99
North Wales (pb)	1-85937-298-8	£9.99	Villages of Devon (pb)	1-85937-293-7	£9.99
North Yorkshire (pb)	1-85937-236-8	£9.99	Villages of Kent (pb)	1-85937-294-5	£9.99
Norwich (pb)	1-85937-194-9	£8.99	Villages of Sussex (pb)	1-85937-295-3	£9.99
Nottingham (pb)	1-85937-324-0	£9.99	Warwickshire (pb)	1-85937-203-1	£9.99
Nottinghamshire (pb)	1-85937-187-6	£9.99	Welsh Castles (pb)	1-85937-322-4	£9.99
Oxford (pb)	1-85937-411-5	£9.99	West Midlands (pb)	1-85937-289-9	£9.99
Oxfordshire (pb)	1-85937-430-1	£9.99	West Sussex	1-85937-148-5	£14.99
Peak District (pb)	1-85937-280-5	£9.99	West Yorkshire (pb)	1-85937-201-5	£9.99
Penzance	1-85937-069-1	£12.99	Weymouth (pb)	1-85937-209-0	£9.99
Peterborough (pb)	1-85937-219-8	£9.99	Wiltshire (pb)	1-85937-277-5	£9.99
Piers	1-85937-237-6	£17.99	Wiltshire Churches (pb)	1-85937-171-x	£9.99
Plymouth	1-85937-119-1	£12.99	Wiltshire Living Memories	1-85937-245-7	£14.99
Poole & Sandbanks (pb)	1-85937-251-1	£9.99	Winchester (pb)	1-85937-428-x	£9.99
Preston (pb)	1-85937-212-0	£9.99	Windmills & Watermills	1-85937-242-2	£17.99
Reading (pb)	1-85937-238-4	£9.99	Worcester (pb)	1-85937-165-5	£9.99
Romford (pb)	1-85937-319-4	£9.99	Worcestershire	1-85937-152-3	£14.99
Salisbury (pb)	1-85937-239-2	£9.99	York (pb)	1-85937-199-x	£9.99
Scarborough (pb)	1-85937-379-8	£9.99	Yorkshire (pb)	1-85937-186-8	£9.99
St Albans (pb)	1-85937-341-0	£9.99	Yorkshire Living Memories	1-85937-166-3	£14.99

See Frith books on the internet www.francisfrith.co.uk

FRITH PRODUCTS & SERVICES

Francis Frith would doubtless be pleased to know that the pioneering publishing venture he started in 1860 still continues today. A hundred and forty years later, The Francis Frith Collection continues in the same innovative tradition and is now one of the foremost publishers of vintage photographs in the world. Some of the current activities include:

Interior Decoration

Today Frith's photographs can be seen framed and as giant wall murals in thousands of pubs, restaurants, hotels, banks, retail stores and other public buildings throughout the country. In every case they enhance the unique local atmosphere of the places they depict and provide reminders of gentler days in an increasingly busy and frenetic world.

Product Promotions

Frith products are used by many major companies to promote the sales of their own products or to reinforce their own history and heritage. Frith promotions have been used by Hovis bread, Courage beers, Scots Porage Oats, Colman's mustard, Cadbury's foods, Mellow Birds coffee, Dunhill pipe tobacco, Guinness, and Bulmer's Cider.

Genealogy and Family History

As the interest in family history and roots grows world-wide, more and more people are turning to Frith's photographs of Great Britain for images of the towns, villages and streets where their ancestors lived; and, of course, photographs of the churches and chapels where their ancestors were christened, married and buried are an essential part of every genealogy tree and family album.

Frith Products

All Frith photographs are available Framed or just as Mounted Prints and Posters (size 23 x 16 inches). These may be ordered from the address below. From time to time other products - Address Books, Calendars, Table Mats, etc - are available.

The Internet

Already twenty thousand Frith photographs can be viewed and purchased on the internet through the Frith websites and a myriad of partner sites.

For more detailed information on Frith companies and products, look at these sites:

www.francisfrith.co.uk
www.francisfrith.com
(for North American visitors)

See the complete list of Frith Books at:

www.francisfrith.co.uk

This web site is regularly updated with the latest list of publications from the Frith Book Company. If you wish to buy books relating to another part of the country that your local bookshop does not stock, you may purchase on-line.

For further information, trade, or author enquiries please contact us at the address below:
The Francis Frith Collection, Frith's Barn, Teffont, Salisbury, Wiltshire, England SP3 5QP.
Tel: +44 (0)1722 716 376 Fax: +44 (0)1722 716 881   Email: sales@francisfrith.co.uk

See Frith books on the internet www.francisfrith.co.uk

TO RECEIVE YOUR **FREE** MOUNTED PRINT

Mounted Print
Overall size 14 x 11 inches

Cut out this Voucher and return it with your remittance for £1.95 to cover postage and handling, to UK addresses. For overseas addresses please include £4.00 post and handling. Choose any photograph included in this book. Your SEPIA print will be A4 in size, and mounted in a cream mount with burgundy rule line, overall size 14 x 11 inches.

Order additional Mounted Prints at HALF PRICE (only £7.49 each*)

If there are further pictures you would like to order, possibly as gifts for friends and family, purchase them at half price (no additional postage and handling required).

Have your Mounted Prints framed*

For an additional £14.95 per print you can have your chosen Mounted Print framed in an elegant polished wood and gilt moulding, overall size 16 x 13 inches (no additional postage and handling required).

---

* IMPORTANT!
These special prices are only available if ordered using the original voucher on this page (no copies permitted) and at the same time as your free Mounted Print, for delivery to the same address

---

Frith Collectors' Guild

From time to time we publish a magazine of news and stories about Frith photographs and further special offers of Frith products. If you would like 12 months FREE membership, please return this form.

Send completed forms to:
The Francis Frith Collection, Frith's Barn, Teffont, Salisbury, Wiltshire SP3 5QP

Voucher for **FREE** and Reduced Price Frith Prints

Picture no.	Page number	Qty	Mounted @ £7.49	Framed + £14.95	Total Cost
		1	**Free of charge***	£	£
			£7.49	£	£
			£7.49	£	£
			£7.49	£	£
			£7.49	£	£
			£7.49	£	£

Please allow 28 days for delivery	*** Post & handling**	**£1.95**
Book Title	**Total Order Cost**	**£**

Please do not photocopy this voucher. Only the original is valid, so please cut it out and return it to us.

I enclose a cheque / postal order for £ . . . . made payable to 'The Francis Frith Collection' OR please debit my Mastercard / Visa / Switch / Amex card *(credit cards please on all overseas orders)*

Number . . . .

Issue No(Switch only) . . . . .Valid from (Amex/Switch) . . . .

Expires . . . . Signature . . . .

Name Mr/Mrs/Ms . . . .

Address . . . .

. . . .

. . . . Postcode . . . .

Daytime Tel No . . . .

The Francis Frith Collectors' Guild

Please enrol me as a member for 12 months free of charge.

Name Mr/Mrs/Ms . . . .

Address . . . .

. . . .

. . . . Postcode . . . .

Would you like to find out more about Francis Frith?

We have recently recruited some entertaining speakers who are happy to visit local groups, clubs and societies to give an illustrated talk documenting Frith's travels and photographs. If you are a member of such a group and are interested in hosting a presentation, we would love to hear from you.

Our speakers bring with them a small selection of our local town and county books, together with sample prints. They are happy to take orders. A small proportion of the order value is donated to the group who have hosted the presentation. The talks are therefore an excellent way of fundraising for small groups and societies.

Can you help us with information about any of the Frith photographs in this book?

We are gradually compiling an historical record for each of the photographs in the Frith archive. It is always fascinating to find out the names of the people shown in the pictures, as well as insights into the shops, buildings and other features depicted.

If you recognize anyone in the photographs in this book, or if you have information not already included in the author's caption, do let us know. We would love to hear from you, and will try to publish it in future books or articles.

Our production team

Frith books are produced by a small dedicated team at offices in the converted Grade II listed 18th-century barn at Teffont near Salisbury, illustrated above. Most have worked with the Frith Collection for many years. All have in common one quality: they have a passion for the Frith Collection. The team is constantly expanding, but currently includes:

Jason Buck, John Buck, Douglas Burns, Heather Crisp, Isobel Hall, Rob Hames, Hazel Heaton, Peter Horne, James Kinnear, Tina Leary, Hannah Marsh, Eliza Sackett, Terence Sackett, Sandra Sanger, Shelley Tolcher, Susanna Walker, Clive Wathen and Jenny Wathen.

Free Print - see overleaf